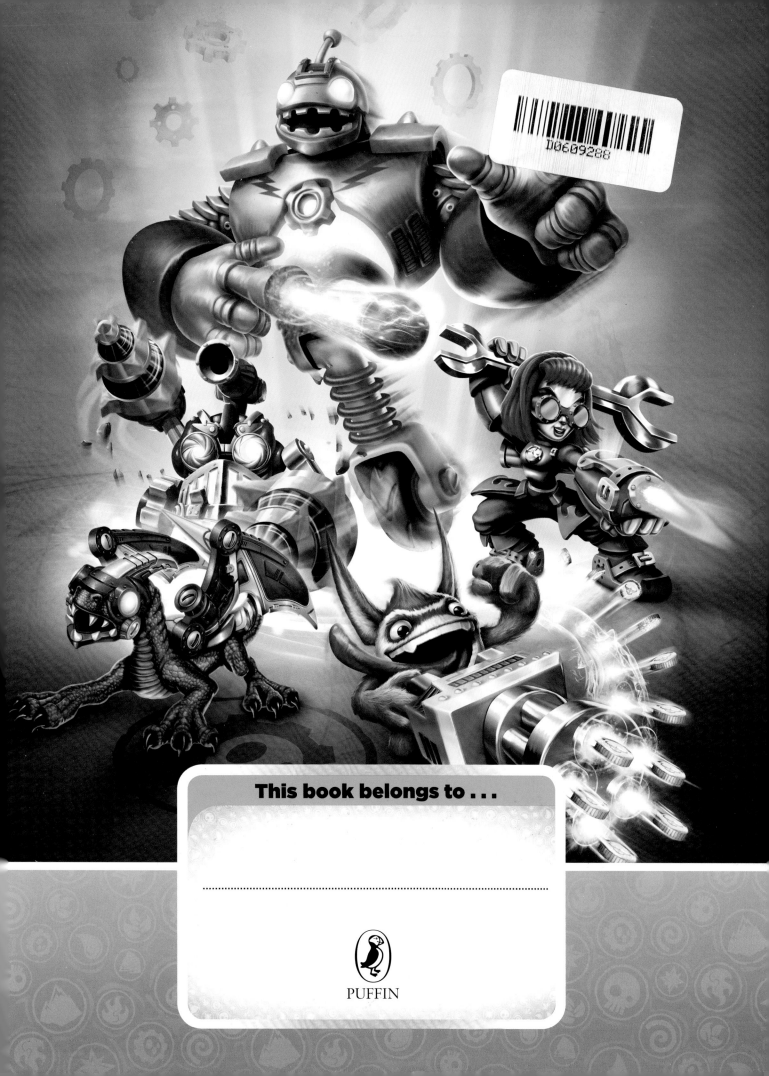

This book belongs to . . .

....

PUFFIN

Published by Puffin 2013
A Penguin Company
Penguin Books Ltd, 80 Strand, London, WC2R 0RL, UK
Penguin Group (USA) Inc., 375 Hudson Street, New York 10014, USA
Penguin Books Australia Ltd, 707 Collins Street, Melbourne, Victoria 3008,
Australia (A division of Pearson Australia Group Pty Ltd)
Canada, India, New Zealand, South Africa

Written by Cavan Scott
Stories illustrated by Dani Geremia – Beehive Illustration Agency
Comic illustrated by Diego Diaz

www.puffinbooks.com

ISBN: 978-1-40939-204-0
001
Printed in Canada

CONTENTS

SKYLANDS: A VISITOR'S GUIDE

Welcome to Skylands! Made up of an infinite number of floating islands, Skylands is a realm of magic, mystery and often mayhem. Here's some essential information for your visit. Have fun!

ANCIENT HISTORY

Thousands of years ago, Skylands was ruled by an evil race of robotic villains known as the Arkeyans. The Arkeyan King was eventually defeated by the first ever Skylanders – the Giants – but Arkeyan tech and treasure is still buried all over Skylands.

LANDMARKS

The Core of Light shines from the ruins of Master Eon's Citadel. Its brilliant beam keeps the forces of Darkness at bay. Kaos' Kastle is the ancestral seat of the family of Kaos, evil Portal Master and all-round smelly maniac. Voted Worst Decorated Evil Lair three years running.

SKYLANDERS

This band of brave heroes is always on hand to send evil-doers packing. Within their numbers you'll find dragons, robots, storm titans, genies, ice ogres and even a few incredible creatures with swappable tops and bottoms!

Skylands Dos and Don'ts

Don't
Buy antiques from trolls. There's every chance they will explode before you get home.

Do
Use a hot-air balloon to travel between islands.

Don't
Use catapults, cannons or carrier pigeons to travel between islands.

Do
Try Batterson's steak and sheep-wool pie. It's delicious.

WHERE'S ERMIT?

We had hoped Ermit the Hermit would welcome you to this book, but unfortunately the nervous so-and-so spotted some dodgy-looking clouds and did a runner. He's hiding somewhere in the pages that follow. Can you find him?

THE LOCALS

Here are some of the folk you'll find in Skylands . . .

MABU

These furry little fellows can be found all over Skylands. In the face of increased troll activity, these usually timid creatures formed the Mabu Defence Force. Unfortunately, it was a bit rubbish. Luckily, the Skylanders were around to save the day.

NOTABLE MABU: After his home was ravaged by a tornado, Snuckles became the first ever Mabu secret agent.

MOLEKIN

Short-sighted and completely bald, these miners were once blessed with long, luscious locks. Unfortunately they used crude oil as hair tonic, which made all their hair fall out!

NOTABLE MOLEKIN: Crotchety and blind as a bat, Diggs helped the Skylanders rebuild the Core of Light after it was destroyed by Kaos.

GILLMEN

Gillmen hail originally from Oilspill Island. They love to sing – which is unfortunate, as their singing voices are appalling.

NOTABLE GILLMAN: Secretly, Gurglefin has always wanted to be a pirate. Don't tell Gill Grunt.

GHOSTS

On the whole, Skylands' ghosts aren't all that scary. In fact, they're rather sociable. In the past, they used to eat brains, but now they prefer noshing down on pastries and pies.

NOTABLE GHOST: Machine Ghost is a sensitive spirit that haunts Ermit the Hermit's giant Arkeyan robot.

TROLLS

Trolls once lived under bridges and collected tolls. After people realized they were easily fooled by the use of billy goats, the bottom fell out of the toll market so trolls decided to blow things up instead.

NOTABLE TROLL: When Kaos became Emperor of the Arkeyans, he promoted his troll sidekick Glumshanks to Oiling Assistant Third Class. Big deal.

Don't
Drop litter. Instead, throw it into a rubbish bin or, if possible, a passing tornado.

Do
Feel free to blow up sheep. Everyone else does.

True or False?

A team of lazy troll tile-layers invented the game of Skystones.

☐ TRUE ☐ FALSE

ROGUES GALLERY

BOO! HISS! THEY'RE SKYLANDS' BIGGEST BADDIES - AND YOU WOULDN'T WANT TO MEET ANY OF THEM IN A DARK ALLEY. OR A LIGHT ONE, FOR THAT MATTER.

NOODLES
ICE OGRE

"Ha! You fell right into my trap! Except for the part where you destroyed my gifts to the Great Evil Ice Master."

Liked to catch hailstones on his tongue when he was young. Unfortunately, the hailstones were the size of footballs. All sense was soon knocked out of him.

Evil rating	4/10
Strength rating	7/10
Brain rating	2/10
Smell rating	3/10

ARKEYAN CONQUERTRON
GIANT ARKEYAN ROBOT

"Your attempt to destroy me is completely unauthorized."

One of the evil robots that enslaved the Mabu and ruled Skylands 10,000 years ago. Was resurrected by Kaos during the search for the Iron Fist of Arkus.

Evil rating	8/10
Strength rating	10/10
Brain rating	6/10
Smell rating	1/10

CHOMPY MAGE
CHOMPY-OBSESSED WIZARD

"I am the Chompy Mage! And you are not a chompy! So I don't like you."

Madder than a bag of Bone Chompies, this one. A sorcerer who dresses like a Chompy, has a pet Chompy glove puppet and can transform into a giant, mutant Chompy.

Evil rating	4/10
Strength rating	7/10
Brain rating	2/10
Smell rating	3/10

DID YOU KNOW?
Like Flynn, the Chompy Mage loves enchiladas. Unlike Flynn, he eats them while dressed in full Chompy costume.

8

DRILL-X
GIGANTIC DRILLING ROBOT

"It's the end of the track, Sky-lander!
This drill-bot is on the scene.
I'll-knock-you forward and back,
With a robo-a-tack,Coz you're messin'
with the wrong ma-cheeeeen!"

Kaos' drilling robot is feared wherever he goes – not because of his razor-sharp drill-bits, but because of his screeching singing. It sounds like gears grinding together!

Evil rating 7/10
Strength rating 9/10
Brain rating... 5/10
Smell rating 2/10

PIPSQUEAK
CYCLOPS ARENA MASTER

Excellent! A Skylander!
Fun, fun, fun!"

Cowardly and weak, this is one cyclops with an eye for trouble. Sets up battle arenas and is amazed when the Skylanders beat his champions every time. Silly!

Evil rating 4/10
Strength rating.......................................1/10
Brain rating...4/10
Smell rating 9/10

KAOS
EVIL PORTAL MASTER EXTRAORDINAIRE

"BEHOLD! It is I, Kaos,
and as you can see,
I AM AWESOME!!!!"

The most evil creature ever to be born. Will stop at nothing to take over Skylands. So cruel, wicked, hateful, repulsive, stinking, villainous and vile that words fail us.

Evil rating 10/10
Strength rating.......................................2/10
Brain rating...8/10
Smell rating 10/10

BRUTE
KAOS' PRIZE FIGHTER

"I'm just getting warmed up
here. INCREASE THE PAIN!"

A champion jaw-breaker, Brute is slow with his wits but quick with his feet. His secret desire is to go on a lovely fishing trip with his master, Kaos.

Evil rating 7/10
Strength rating.................................. 8/10
Brain rating.. 4/10
Smell rating 4/10

SHADOW MASTER

"Be afraid foolish fools. I, KAOS, have unleashed an army of swarming shadow clones. The only way to beat them is to work out which shadow perfectly matches ME! You are DOOOOOMED!!!"

A   B

C   D

True or False?
True or False?

Kaos' family used to make their own soda. The flavours included sand, mud, and radioactive suction eel.

☐ TRUE   ☐ FALSE

Total Kaos

by Onk Beakman

"What are YOU doing here?" Spyro roared, smoke billowing from his nostrils. Behind the dragon, Chop Chop had drawn his sword and dropped into an attack position.

Zook couldn't believe what was happening. He'd been enjoying a snooze beneath the Core of Light when he'd heard Spyro and Chop Chop approaching. He'd got up to say hello and Spyro had gone crazy.

"What are you talking about? It's just me, Zoo-OOF!" Zook gasped as Spyro leapt forward, pinning him to the ground.

The dragon loomed over the confused bambazooker, snarling in Zook's face. "You've got some nerve, Kaos!"

"Kaos?" spluttered Zook. "What are you talking about? I'm . . ." His voice trailed off as he caught his reflection in Chop Chop's raised weapon. A face was staring back at him – a face that wasn't his own!

"I look like Kaos!" he cried out, wondering if he was still dreaming. But no, Spyro's claws felt real enough.

"Of course you look like Kaos," Spyro growled. "You *are* Kaos!"

"No, I'm not. I'm Zook. I don't know what's going on."

"Hey, what's happening?" rumbled a deep voice. It was Tree Rex, thundering over to see what the problem was. The Giant's face twisted into a snarl when he saw who was trapped beneath Spyro's claws.

"Kaos! How did he get here?"

"He says he's Zook," explained Chop Chop. "It's obviously a trick."

Before Zook could argue, Chop Chop was enveloped in a flash of sickly green light.

When it cleared, the skeletal guard was gone, replaced by a small, hunched figure. No, that was impossible. It was another Kaos, still wielding the Arkeyan blade!

A second later, the same thing happened to Spyro. There was a burst of light and – *FOOM!* – a perfect copy of Kaos appeared, crouching over Zook in Spyro's place.

"What's happening to us?" spluttered the Kaos who had been Chop Chop.

"No idea," said Zook, "but do you believe me now?"

"I don't know what to believe," said the Kaos who had been Spyro, releasing his grip on Zook and looking around in horror.

All over the Ruins, Skylanders were transforming into perfect duplicates of Kaos: *FOOM! FOOM! FOOM!*

Even Tree Rex transformed into a gigantic version of the Portal Master.

Arguments immediately began breaking out between the transformed Skylanders, all bickering in Kaos' whiny voice.

Above them, Eon's concerned face shimmered into view. "Calm yourselves," the spirit pleaded. "This is just one of Kaos' spells. He is here. I can sense him. He wishes to destroy the Core of Light from within."

The Kaos who had been Spyro looked around at the crowd of identical evil Portal Masters. "But how do we know who is the real Kaos? He could be any of us!"

An idea struck Zook. What would the real Kaos be doing right now? Boasting, that's what!

"I'M the real Kaos," he suddenly announced, puffing out his chest in mock pride. "This is MY brilliant plan. You are all DOOMED!"

A frown passed over the Chop Chop Kaos' face. "But you said you were . . . oh!" The guard smiled, realizing what Zook was doing. "No, I am Kaos," he shouted theatrically. "This is all MY doing!"

"Don't be stupid," snapped Spyro, winking at Zook. "I'm the real deal. I'm Kaos!"

Catching on quickly, the rest of the Skylanders joined in, all claiming they were the genuine article. Zook grinned. This would drive the real Kaos nuts!

They didn't have to wait long . . .

"NO, you FOOLS!" screeched a voice. The Skylanders turned to see a lone Kaos standing by the Core of Light, his ugly face flushed with anger. "I am Kaos! Only a GENIUS like me could devise such a cunning plan."

Another Kaos shuffled forward, wringing his hands with worry. "Master, what are you doing?" he snivelled, as the furious Kaos threw his hands into the air.

"Only a Portal Master as powerful as ME could cast the Despicable Duplication Spell of DOOOOM," he crowed.

"Don't believe you," sneered Zook. "Prove it."

"My pleasure, Skyblunderer. BEHOLD!" He clapped his pudgy hands together and one by one the Skylanders all returned to normal.

"SEE?" bellowed the real Kaos as the cringing duplicate beside him changed back into Glumshanks. "I am KAOS, the greatest Portal Master Skylands has ever known, and —"

"— completely surrounded," snivelled Glumshanks.

Kaos' face fell as he realized that his butler was right. Every Skylander's weapon was trained on him.

"CURSES!" Kaos yelped, snapping his fingers together. "Until next time, SKYLOSERS!"

And with that, Kaos and Glumshanks were gone.

A cheer went up across the Ruins.

"Well done, Zook!" said Eon with a smile. "That was quick thinking."

"Ah, it was no biggie," the Bambazooker chuckled as the Skylanders crowded around him. "We did it together."

"Master Eon's right," Spyro laughed, slapping Zook on the back. "I don't know about Kaos, but you're definitely one of a kind!"

The End

BOUNCER
"Deal with the wheel!"

SPORT ROBOTO BALL

ORIGIN
Thousands of years ago, Bouncer was an All-Star Roboto Ball player. In fact, he was the most famous Roboto Ball player in all of Skylands. He couldn't go anywhere without being mobbed by fans. However, the rise of the Arkeyan Empire spelled the end of Roboto Ball. Bouncer's hometown was destroyed and he was converted into a security bot.

HOW DID HE BECOME A SKYLANDER?
Even though they were being forced to work in Arkeyan mines, the Mabu remembered Bouncer from his Roboto Ball days. When he realized how much his fans still loved him, Bouncer couldn't bear to just stand by and see them oppressed. So he joined the Skylanders and battled the Arkeyan King.

PERSONALITY
Talk about being larger than life! Bouncer is one of the most upbeat Skylanders you'll meet. Always bursting with energy, he's fast-talking and a real live wire.

SPECIAL ABILITIES
Bouncer can fire bouncy balls from his fingertips and blast I-beams from his eyes. Those shoulder pads aren't just a funky fashion statement either – they hide rocket launchers.

DID YOU KNOW?
One of the most exciting things about Roboto Ball is that the balls themselves often exploded for no good reason. While this made for exciting games on the pitch, it caused havoc when the players practised at home.

SPORT STARS
Before they were Skylanders, some of Eon's champions were sporting heroes...

FLAMESLINGER
"Let the flames begin!"

SPORT ARCHERY

ORIGIN
When folk first saw Flameslinger score a bullseye, they thought he was showing off. He was wearing a blindfold, after all. Little did they know that this fiery elf could see through flames.

DID YOU KNOW?
His enchanted flame bow and blistering shoes were given to him after he saved a fire spirit from drowning in a forest lake.

HOW DID HE BECOME A SKYLANDER?
Eon is quite the sport fan, you know. He was present when Flameslinger won the Skylands archery contest by setting fire to all of the targets (and his competitors' arrows to boot!)

SPECIAL ABILITIES
Flameslinger can fire flaming arrows at his foes. There's no getting away from him either. He runs so fast, he sets the ground on fire.

SPORT BOXING

ORIGIN
When it came to jousting, no one could beat Fright Rider and his spectacular ostrich, Ozzy. After winning their third championship in a row, a jealous rival cast a spell that transported Fright Rider to the Land of the Undead. The naturally nervous Ozzy swallowed his courage – and an entire bag of skele-oats – and transformed into an Undead skeleton. He charged into the Undead realm to save his elven friend, and the rest is Skylands history!

HOW DID HE BECOME A SKYLANDER?
Fright Rider was so touched by his steed's sacrifice that he dedicated his life to fighting evil (although they still joust from time to time).

PERSONALITY
Gallant and brave, Fright Rider is always ready to rush headlong into action.

DID YOU KNOW?
Ozzy still sticks his head in the ground . . . but only to burrow beneath his foes and attack.

FRIGHT RIDER
"Fear the spear!"

SPECIAL ABILITIES
Enemies will soon get the point of Fright Rider's bone-hard spear.

TERRAFIN
"It's feeding time!"

SPORT BOXING

ORIGIN
Terrafin once trained as a lifeguard, but he was put out of business when Kaos transformed the Dirt Seas into a vast sheet of glass. Never one to give up, the Dirt Shark became a boxer and was soon knocking his rivals out of the ring. The only problem was, soon there were no other fighters left.

DID YOU KNOW?
Terrafin was the Skylander who discovered Drill Sergeant, buried deep underground.

HOW DID HE BECOME A SKYLANDER?
Master Eon was in the crowd at his last bout, and needed a heavyweight for his new band of Skylanders. Terrafin nearly bit the Portal Master's hand off when he asked (not literally!).

SPECIAL ABILITIES
This toothy brawler can dive beneath the ground, swim through the soil and then burst up to deliver a knockout blow.

SPORT LIGHTNING BOLT TOSS

ORIGIN
For years, Lightning Rod dominated the annual Storm Titan games, winning trophy after trophy. He was so popular that soon the Cloud Kingdom became littered with statues of the muscle-bound hunk. All that changed, however, during the final of the triple gold ring lightning bolt toss with a twist. Kaos' Giant Floating Head appeared above the stadium, demanding that the Storm Titans join his dark armies.

DID YOU KNOW?
Lightning Rod's autobiography - Rod the Bod - has sold over one million copies (although he did buy a lot of them himself).

HOW DID HE BECOME A SKYLANDER?
Quick as a flash (of lightning), Rod chucked his bolt through the huge head, shocking the real Kaos – literally. Master Eon awarded Rod his biggest prize by making him a Skylander there and then.

LIGHTNING ROD
"One strike and you're out!"

SPECIAL ABILITIES
Rod can chuck lightning and control thunderclouds – all while pulling the perfect heroic pose.

True or False?
Flameslinger used Chompies for target practice when he was little.
☐ **TRUE** ☐ **FALSE**

SKYLANDER SEARCH

IT'S TIME TO TEST YOUR SKYLANDERS KNOWLEDGE. HAVE A GO AT THE QUESTIONS ON THE RIGHT AND THEN FIND THE ANSWERS HIDDEN AWAY IN THE GRID. HAPPY SEARCHING!

```
F F W R L L M I K E S T O U T K Y O F L Y T S S C Q Z C A M
L T K R V H U C N A M H S K C A M R D U U N L U O I U F M H
A X B P E J P J W O D R G I L L G R U N T A A K R U P E V I
S N A Q B C W L O I E T H C A Y D A E R D E M R E L T A W Z
H S I N N U K B J T S E N O T S Y K S D E G B A O W J N W K
W C K C H A M I S I U Z T X Q W G L J L X R A M F O P R C I
I T T G U O M A N N E T D W S B V L H W J E M L L W Y F V S
N E M H O Q M V V G P O C A V A N N K A V S V V I A I B O O
G T U R U L H N W Y B T W H N O R N Z R N L F T G Z N O O N
S K H U A M V K V M E A O N M U S S U B P L S T H A I B D I
Y S A T V I P Y X K I L L R A N E K Y E J I A J T C R R O C
N O R V C H L B C X X Y A L Z A K H R Y D R T T B D X O O B
S O P G G O L O A X A I V X Z T X C G E K D Y I K T H F D O
P Q F M F F R O L C P M T K I I N S A V W B K A O Y F S X O
B A B L K P W H A F K C Y E M T H O R D U M M E U B I Y U M
S D L X S W N U O Z G P C N L M A G T M C S J A N G J O A A
O Q T D V I M Q J V V J W E I R J V P E A A Z E M E X T S K
A Y E V L X V P F K X T X E J O D O W N L M O R S M W Z J A
X G A R Y P A N T O N O G Y D T V F B I K E A U R I C W O T
T R I G G E R H A P P Y D J I S M N W Q L D K T Q C T N T O
F P I Q V T K K X M O B W R D G G N W F A A M S I Y W C E R
C G D O K W E A O F Z I R V A P Q M I L B V X I N I J N I N
S J U I P S G D J N X Y J S F E S Y D I C T E I H P L U R Z
D S F O A J N O B I D E M S S U B H E S U X N W N A L Q T S
O T H Y T R B Z D U O Y C N C L P D A B H C Q F I A L J J J
X E R E E R T A C T Y R F O O L H K A G L I M Q P L R A C T
M G J K G B Y E S L O X G I T E M F M E P X A Z O B I R P P
N Y Q N A D C Z D R N H C T T F M T Q H R F X N B B I K J W
O Z A C X L H F Z D W U O O W B C F T F O D M Z J Q S V I C
O N K B E A K M A N U P I P B O O M E R G C T B O I V S F N
```

1 The Portal Master who taught Eon everything he knows (10)

_ _ _ _ _ _ _ _ _ _

2 Fright Rider's ostrich is one of these (8)

_ _ _ _ _ _ _ _

3 Terrafin found this Arkeyan Skylander snoozing underground (5,8)

_ _ _ _ _ _ _ _ _ _ _ _ _

4 Pop Fizz mixes these (7)

_ _ _ _ _ _ _

5 A Gillman who fell in love with a mermaid (4,5)

_ _ _ _ _ _ _ _ _

6 Followers of the Darkness will hope they never meet this magical Giant (7)

_ _ _ _ _ _ _

7 An Air Skylander who flattens enemies by screaming at them (5,4)

_ _ _ _ _ _ _ _ _

8 The scurviest pirate captain of them all (10)

_ _ _ _ _ _ _ _ _ _

9 This Tech Skylander loves her Bouncing Betty Mines (8)

_ _ _ _ _ _ _ _

10 A Giant who has a whale of a time (9)

_ _ _ _ _ _ _ _ _

11 Magical Arkeyan pollution created this defender of forests (4,3)

_ _ _ _ _ _ _

12 A game played throughout Skylands (9)

_ _ _ _ _ _ _ _ _

13 The device that holds the Darkness at bay (4,2,5)

_ _ _ _ _ _ _ _ _ _ _

14 A fiery little mutt (3,3)

_ _ _ _ _ _

15 Both Eon and Kaos are these (as are you!) (6,7)

_ _ _ _ _ _ _ _ _ _ _ _ _

16 A toadstool paratrooper (10)

_ _ _ _ _ _ _ _ _ _

17 This heroic grub will eat anything (8,4)

_ _ _ _ _ _ _ _ _ _ _ _

18 Lightning Rod is one (5,5)

_ _ _ _ _ _ _ _ _ _

19 A Giant who is actually made up of two separate Skylanders (3,5)

_ _ _ _ _ _ _ _

20 The lost city of the ancient Arkeyans (5)

_ _ _ _ _

21 A banker who sells Skylanders new treasures and tools (5)

_ _ _ _ _

22 Flynn's cursed ship (5,5)

_ _ _ _ _ _ _ _ _ _

23 The Skylander with the golden guns (7,5)

_ _ _ _ _ _ _ _ _ _ _ _

24 A beautiful gem dragon (9)

_ _ _ _ _ _ _ _ _

25 This Skylander is "Armed and Dangerous" (4,3)

_ _ _ _ _ _ _

26 Kaos' childhood wooden friends (7)

_ _ _ _ _ _ _

ALL ABOARD
THE DREAD-YACHT!

Well, hello! This is Flynn, your devastatingly handsome captain, welcoming you aboard the Dread-Yacht, the fastest, bestest ship in all of Skylands. Ain't she a beaut? Almost as impressive as yours truly. Let me show you around . . .

STEERING WHEEL
Where the magic happens. Skylands' best pilot* is happiest when he's behind the wheel, ready to sail into adventure.

*Er, that's me by the way.

GUN DECK
Trigger Happy's favourite place on the ship. He's always down there firing away – even if there aren't any enemies to shoot at!

THE GALLEY
I always keep the galley stocked with enchiladas. In fact, I keep enchiladas all over the ship in case of emergencies. Oh look – here's one in my boot. Yum!

CALI'S CABIN

Cali spends hours locked up in here (probably trying to pluck up the courage to ask me out on a date, I'll bet). The poor gal is just crazy about me. Hey, it's easy to see why. Boom!

OCTOPHONIC MUSIC PLAYER

This musical thingamawhatsit should be able to play every song ever composed. Unfortunately, it got stuck and plays the same tune over and over and over again. It's driving me ker-razy! Must get Sprocket to fix it some day.

DINGHY

This handy little lander's got me out of some real scrapes. Like the time I had to make a swift exit from Buccaneer Beach. I didn't mean to crash the Pirate Princess's ship into the side of that crystal cliff. The steering must have been off . . .

THE GAMES ROOM

You can play all sorts here. Anything your heart desires. Well, as long as your heart desires a game of Skystones, that is.

FLYNN'S CABIN

Home of the legendary Visiagram, a clever doohicky that lets me give the Dread-Yacht a magical make-over from time to time. Also where I keep my collection of mirrors. Never tire of gazing into them. Sigh!

OUTBOARD MOTOR

The Dread-Yacht used to be powered by a family of angry raccoons. Why were they angry? No idea. Something about only being fed Brussels sprout sandwiches between shifts. Anyhoo, we've replaced them with a brand new motor. Well, nearly new.

"You wouldn't believe what I paid for the Dread-Yacht – it was a real bargain! The guy who sold her to me seemed pretty desperate to get rid of her, actually. I can still hear him laughing hysterically as he grabbed the money and ran. Of course, some folk think that she's cursed, but I don't know why. It's not like bits of her are always breaking down or anything. Hey, what's that? The aft rudder's broken down? Again? What are the chances?"

LETHAL LABYRINTH

FLASHWING IS ON HER WAY TO HELP BASH BATTLE A GRUESOME GARGANTULA. CAN YOU GUIDE HER THROUGH THE WEB-FILLED MAZE? YOU CAN PASS THROUGH THE WEBS, BUT AVOID THE SCUTTLING SPIDERLINGS. SHUDDER!

DID YOU KNOW?

Flashwing arrived in Skylands the day Bash made a wish that he could fly. She streaked out of the sky like a shooting star. Bash immediately lost his heart to the beautiful gem dragon, but then lost a few scales as she blasted him with a laser pulse from her tail. Whoops!

EXIT

20

NEW YEAR'S RESOLUTIONS

Some of the Skylanders have promised to turn over a new leaf for the New Year.
Rate their chances of sticking to their New Year's resolutions.

HOT DOG

"I'll stop trying to bury Chop Chop under Master Eon's vegetable patch. The trouble is, those bones look so tasty. Ruff ruff!"

LIGHTNING ROD

"I promise to be a little more humble this year, which will be easy as I am so very brilliant. And strong. And, let's face it, handsome."

ZAP

"I promise not to electrocute dolphins while I race against them. Unless it happens by accident, of course."

SPYRO

"I'll think before I rush head first into danger."

STUMP SMASH

"I'll try to be more patient with trolls. Just because they cut down my forest, chopped off my branches and are thoroughly detestable doesn't mean they deserve to be flattened beneath my hammers, right?"

TRIGGER HAPPY

"I will ask questions first and shoot later. Or is it shoot first, ask questions later? Ah, who needs questions? Pow pow pow!"

ERUPTOR

"I promise to keep my cool and not blow my top. What do you mean I'll never be able to do it? Why I oughta . . ."

WRECKING BALL

"I'll go on a diet. Burp!"

KAOS

"I promise never to try to take over Skylands ever again. HA! Only joking. You are all DOOOOOOOOOOOOOMED!"

WHAT'S YOUR RESOLUTION?

Do you stand more chance of keeping your New Year's Resolution? Write it here and check back at the end of the year to see how you did.

This year I promise to . . .

_____

_____

_____

EGG-RUPTOR!

Heat up breakfast time with this super-hot Eruptor egg cup. Just make sure he doesn't boil over!

YOU WILL NEED

- A pack of air-hardening clay
- A clay-modelling tool
- An egg (a hard-boiled one is best)
- A toothpick
- Acrylic paints and paintbrushes

1. Cut a chunk of clay from the block and mould it into a base for Eruptor. Pinch the sides to make it look like lava is flowing down, but make sure the top is left flat.

2. Put the base aside and take two smaller chunks of clay. Roll them into thick sausages and cut off the ends so they're flat. These will become Eruptor's legs.

3. Dip the bottom of the legs in water and, after also getting the top of the base slightly wet, stick them in place.

4. Get a ball of clay and push your thumbs into the middle to make the egg cup. Use the egg to see if it's big enough. Then attach the egg cup to the legs using water. Make sure it's stuck on well.

Egg pops in here

5. Make two more sausages of clay. Each needs to have one rounded end and a flat end, like this.

6. Wet the flat ends and stick them to the sides of the egg cup. These are Eruptor's arms. Curl one of them up so it holds the egg in place. Add little spikes of clay to his shoulders to make Eruptor's spikes.

7. Take a toothpick and carefully mark the clay of Eruptor's body to give him a molten-rock look.

8. Check the egg fits one more time and then leave for 24 hours to dry.

9. Once your egg cup is completely dry, give Eruptor a lick of paint. Use red paint for his body and base, and yellow for his hands and feet. You could even paint an eggshell to look like his face!

flat end

Remember to ask for an adult's permission before creating Egg-Ruptor, and don't try to boil the egg on your own!

23

TERRAFIN

LIGHTNING ROD

HOT DOG

SHROOMBOOM

JET-VAC

HOME SWEET HOME

The Skylanders hail from all over Skylands. Can you match the hero with their original home?

SWARM

CHILL

DID YOU KNOW?
Eon found out he could use Portals when he accidentally transported his master into the middle of the Dirt Seas.

Dirt Seas

Windham

Popcorn Volcano

Kaos' Pizza Topping Garden

The Honeycomb Pyramid

Cloud Kingdom

The Ice Kingdom

ONK BEAKMAN'S EYE-OPENING CYCLOPS FACTS

SKYLANDS' CELEBRATED WRITER AND ISLAND-HOPPER TAKES A LOOK AT THE ONE-EYED MENACES . . .

1 Unlike most of Skylands' more nasty critters, cyclopses are actually quite artistic. They are phenomenal stonemasons. In my travels I've seen hundreds, no thousands, no millions of their stone castles, temples and statues.

2 Unfortunately, while their buildings are spectacular, cyclopses aren't known for their brains. They once carved an entire armada of stone sailing ships. The Cyclops Lord Admiral launched the fleet, only to see them sink within seconds.

3 The failure of the Stone Navy didn't stop the dim-witted fellows. They later went on to attempt to build stone hot-air balloons. The idea didn't get off the ground.

4 Cyclopses have no noses. How do they smell? Terrible! Ha, ha, ha. That tickled me. Of course, all joking aside, they really do reek.

5 The smell gets even worse in the heat, so it's a good thing that so many cyclopses live in extremely cold places. Brrrr.

6 In days gone by, the snowclopses of the Ice Kingdom spent most of their time trying to capture the Ice Queen. Well, everyone needs a hobby.

7 As you'd expect, most cyclopses have only one eye. However, two-eyed biclopses such as Axecutioners do exist.

8 According to legend, there was once a Cyclops Queen who had three eyes. Unfortunately for her, they all looked in different directions.

9 Timidclopses are scared of everything, including their own reflections – which is the reason why mirrors are usually banned in cyclops cities.

10 Cyclopses love their pets. Unfortunately, their pets tend to be ferocious, unruly beasts such as the wild and woolly cyclops mammoths. Even worse are the slobbering mutticuses. The drool from these monsters is one of the stickiest substances in all of Skylands. Mohawk Cyclopses use it to stick their wigs to their heads.

True or False?

Before she became a Skylander, Chill was the protector of the Ice King.

☐ TRUE ☐ FALSE

WHICH DREAD-YACHT CREW MEMBER ARE YOU?

FLYNN'S CREW ARE CERTAINLY A MIXED BAG OF ADVENTURERS, BUT
WHICH ONE DO YOU HAVE THE MOST IN COMMON WITH?
TAKE OUR QUIZ TO FIND OUT . . .

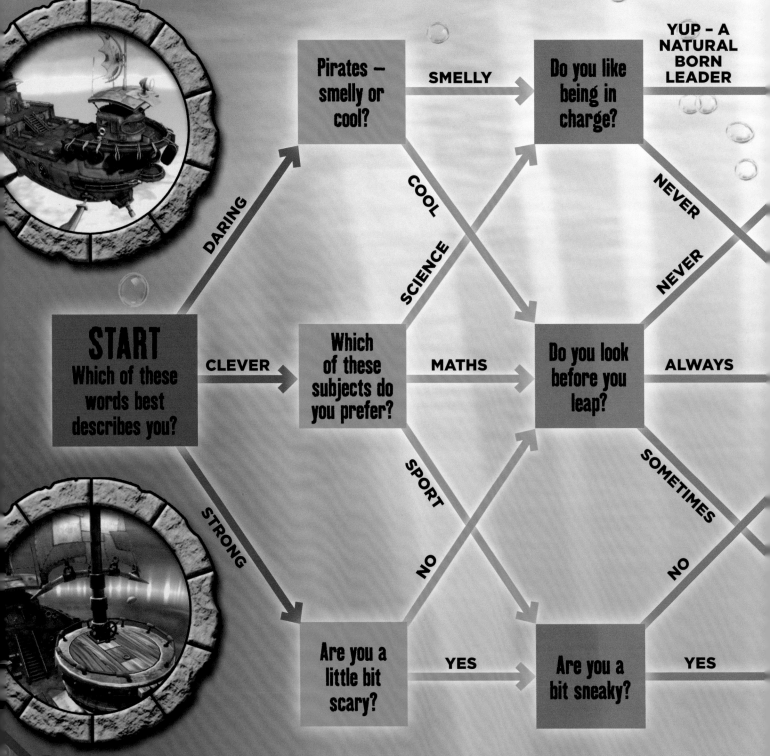

START
Which of these words best describes you?

DARING → Pirates – smelly or cool?

SMELLY → Do you like being in charge? → YUP – A NATURAL BORN LEADER

COOL

CLEVER → Which of these subjects do you prefer?

SCIENCE

MATHS → Do you look before you leap?

NEVER

NEVER

ALWAYS

SPORT

STRONG → Are you a little bit scary?

YES → Are you a bit sneaky?

SOMETIMES

NO

NO

YES

You are like **CALI.** A former explorer, smart and sassy Cali now helps to train the Skylanders. She has quite a soft spot for Flynn, but would never let him know that.

NO, YOU CAN ALWAYS IMPROVE

You are like **FLYNN.** Brave, handsome and devastatingly modest, Flynn is Skylands' greatest pilot ever. Well, according to himself at least. BOOM!

Are you perfect in just about every way?

OF COURSE!

You are like **PERSEPHONE**
A lifelong friend of the Skylanders who is always flitting about. This quirky fairy can provide magical upgrades and new powers . . . for a price, of course.

MAGIC POWERS

You are like **AURIC.** Skylands' finest (and indeed only) banker loves gold almost as much as Trigger Happy. He now runs a special store, supplying Skylanders with that little extra.

What would you rather have?

LOADS OF MONEY

You are like **BROCK.** This bruiser floats like a butterfly and stings like a hulking great Goliath Drow. Likes nothing more than organizing fights and contests – when he's not scrapping himself, that is!

NO, LET'S ARM WRESTLE INSTEAD

Do you like playing Skystones?

YES, FANCY A GAME?

You are like **DREADBEARD**
There's one thing this salty sea dog loves even more than pirating, and that's playing games of Skystones. Yarrrr!

F CREATURE FEATURE

BE AFRAID!
THIS PUZZLE IS SWARMING WITH VILLAINS, ENEMIES AND MONSTERS. CAN YOU FIT THEM SAFELY IN THE GRID? THE CRUNCHERS HAVE BEEN ADDED TO START YOU OFF. TAKE YOUR TIME - THIS ONE'S A BIT TRICKY!

4

C R U N

8

1

5

6

One of these characters isn't a bad **guy or** monster at all. **Which one is it?**

8 LETTERS

ARKEYANS
CHOMPIES

4 LETTERS

DROW
KAOS
IMPS

9 LETTERS

BAG O BOOMS
~~CRUNCHERS~~
D RIVETERS
PIPSQUEAK

5 LETTERS

BRUTE
OGRES
HYDRA

10 LETTERS

BARK DEMONS
CHOMPY MAGE
NAUTELOIDS
SPELL PUNKS

6 LETTERS

DRILL X
TROLLS

11 LETTERS

CONQUERTRON
FRIGHTBEARD
SPIDERLINGS

7 LETTERS

CYCLOPS
DRAGONS
NOODLES
QUIGLEY

14 LETTERS

INHUMAN SHIELDS

C H E R S

Write the letters from the numbered squares here to reveal someone close to Kaos.*

1	2	3	4	5	6	7	8	9	10

*Saying that, you wouldn't want to stand too close to Kaos. The smell would be dreadful!

29

KAOS' KASTLE CAPER

YOU'VE RESCUED CALI FROM THE DEPTHS OF KASTLE KAOS, BUT NOW YOU NEED TO GET OUT. PLAY THIS GAME WITH YOUR FRIENDS TO SEE WHO GETS TO FREEDOM FIRST.

5 YOU FIND AN ELEMENTAL GATE. JUMP THROUGH IT TO 9.

6 D RIVETERS CHASE YOU BACK TO THE START.

7

3 YOU BEAT A MOB OF MOHAWK CYCLOPSES. GO FORWARD 1.

4

1

21 STEP ON A TELEPORTER. ROLL YOUR DIE AGAIN. IF YOU ROLL 1, 2, 3 GO FORWARD 2 SPACES. ROLL 4, 5, 6 GO BACK 2 SPACES.

20 STOP OFF TO SHOP AT AURIC'S STORE. MISS A TURN!

2

22

1 START

23

26 HA! TOTALLY SMASH A CHOMPY-BOT 9000. GO FORWARD 3.

27

24 ARCHIBALD THE WILIKIN SHOWS YOU A SECRET PASSAGE. NIP THROUGHT IT TO 38!

25

Instructions

1. Use sweets or coins as counters. Place them on 'start'.
2. Roll a die. Whoever rolls the lowest number goes first (if it's a tie, roll again).
3. Take turns to roll the die and move your counters by the number of spaces shown on the die. Always follow the instructions on the circles.
4. The first person to land on the last circle is the winner! Congrats!

42

41

40 LOCKED DOOR! MISS A TURN WHILE YOU SEARCH FOR A KEY.

43

44 SHROOMBOOM CATAPULTS YOU FORWARD 2 SPACES.

45 BRUTE KNOCKS YOU BACK 3 SPACES. POW!

30

8 SPOT A PORTRAIT OF KAOS WITH A BIG AFRO. AUGH SO MUCH YOU MISS A TURN!

9

10 BRING WILIKINS BACK TO LIFE. GO FORWARD 3.

11 BONE CHOMPIES BITE YOU ON THE BACKSIDE. BACK 2.

12

13

14 USE A BOUNCEPAD TO LEAP TO 18.

15

16 THE WILIKINS HELP YOU DISTRACT A TROLL SQUADRON. GO FORWARD 3 SPACES.

17 ATTACKED BY A SHADOW DUKE. GO BACK 2 SPACES.

18

28 SEND A SPELL PUNK PACKING. FORWARD 1.

29

30 A DROW WITCH CASTS A SPELL ON YOU. BACK 3.

31 RESCUE A GAGGLE OF FRIENDLY GHOSTS. FORWARD 3 SPACES.

32

33 INHUMAN SHIELDS BLOCK YOUR WAY. MISS A TURN WHILE YOU DEFEAT THEM.

34

35

36 PATH BLOCKED BY GIANT SWINGING KNIVES. MISS A TURN UNTIL YOU ROLL A 4 OR MORE.

37 FALL INTO A CHOMPY PIT. BACK 3 SPACES.

38

39 PLAY BUTTERWORTH THE WILIKIN AT KYSTONES AND WIN. FORWARD 2 SPACES.

46

47

48 KAOS SUMMONS A ROCK GOLEM TO FIGHT YOU. MISS A TURN!

49 FALL THROUGH A TRAPDOOR AND TUMBLE ALL THE WAY BACK TO SPACE 4. NOOOOO!

50 YOU'RE FREE!

TECH TILES

FIT THE MIXED-UP TILES INTO THE GRID BELOW TO REVEAL A FACT ABOUT SPROCKET'S PAST. WE'VE STARTED YOU OFF BY PLACING FOUR OF THE TILES. NOW YOU DO THE REST!

USED	W~~HEN~~	~~I~~	WAS	~~A~~	INVENTIONS	HER
SPR~~O~~CKET	GROWING	~~MAD~~	TO	SHE	UNCLE'S	

SPROCKET			FIX			MAD
	WHEN					UP.

DID YOU KNOW?

Sprocket created her amazing robotic suit so that she could save her inventor uncle from Kaos!

CODE NAMES

Can you help Hugo crack this code from Cali? Look at the pictures of the characters. The numbers refer to the letter of their name. For example, Hugo has already worked out that the second letter of Zap's name is A. Find all the letters to reveal where Hugo needs to meet Cali.

4 = _

5 = _

2 = A

1 = _

4 = _

6 = _

7 = _

5 = _

3 = _

9 = _

5 = _

3 = _

The answer is:

POTION PUZZLER

POP FIZZ HAS BEEN MIXING NEW POTIONS. WHICH TWO OF HIS BEASTLY FORMS ARE EXACTLY THE SAME?

DID YOU KNOW?

No one knows what Pop Fizz looked like before he started experimenting with potions. He once created a potion to help him remember, but instead it made him forget how to wash behind his ears. Weird.

a

b

c

d

e

f

g

h

A Day in the Life of
GLUMSHANKS

Dear Diary,

Another glorious day serving Lord Kaos. What an honour. I sometimes wonder what I've done to deserve this . . .

Have a sneak peak at Glumshanks' secret diary . . .

5am

Up early to scrub the Master's Portal of Power. Unfortunately, he didn't notice I was cleaning it when he woke up. Accidentally transported me into the middle of the Crowded Thorn Jungle. Ouch.

6am–8am

Lord Kaos kindly transported me back. Spent an hour pulling thorns out of my arms, legs and ears. Was late preparing the Master's breakfast of evil eggs on evil toast. Got Portalled back to the Thorn Jungle as punishment. Ouch again.

10am

I never want to see another thorn as long as I live. Master busy drawing up plans to take over Skylands, so started on the washing. Been meaning to launder Lord Kaos' socks for ages. Discovered that his pile of dirty socks smells so bad it's mutated into a giant sock golem.

10.05am–12pm

Two hours of being pummelled by a furious sock golem is not a relaxing way to spend a morning. Managed to trap it in the Sodaworks. I'll deal with that later if I remember.

1pm

Made the Master's lunch. Evil soup to start, followed by evil cheese sandwiches and evil rhubarb crumble. (Actually, we'd run out of evil rhubarb so I just used normal rhubarb. Lord Kaos will never notice.)

1.15pm

Lord Kaos noticed. Back to the Thorn Jungle for me. Need to find a new word for 'ouch'.

2pm

The Master took his Giant Floating Head out for a spin. Tried to enslave the Storm Titans – again! Didn't go well. They pelted us with electrified statues of Lightning Rod. One landed right on my foot. Lord Kaos gave up and retreated to Kastle Kaos. Stopped off at Mabu Market for a pint of milk on the way home, so it wasn't a wasted journey.

5.30pm

The Master's dinner time. Didn't want to take any risks this time so made him evil sheep stew with evil dumplings, and evil bread and butter pudding for afters. The Master burned his tongue on the pudding. Guess where I ended up?

5.35pm

Ouch.

7pm

Spent the evening typing up the Master's memoirs: "Kaos – My Family and Other Power-Crazed Dictators". He's dedicated it to his mother. Sweet. Noticed I've not got a mention yet.

Midnight

Was about to go to bed when the master demanded evil sea sludge soda as a nightcap. Off to the Sodaworks I go. Sure there was something I had to remember about the Sodaworks. Ah well, sure it'll come back to me . . .

HAT HUNT

HATS DON'T JUST KEEP YOUR HEAD WARM IN SKYLANDS. THEY GIVE YOU EXTRA POWERS TOO. ORGANISE A HAT-FINDING EXPEDITION WITH THIS HANDY MISSION PLANNER. IT'LL TELL YOU WHICH SKYLANDER WILL JOIN YOU ON YOUR ADVENTURE, WHERE YOU'LL GO, WHICH HAT YOU'LL DISCOVER AND WHICH ENEMY YOU'LL FACE. ALL YOU NEED IS A DIE!

STEP 1 — WHO WILL JOIN YOU?
ROLL THE DIE

| Spyro | Gill Grunt | Terrafin | Eruptor | Whirlwind | Zook |

STEP 2 — WHERE ARE YOU GOING?
ROLL THE DIE

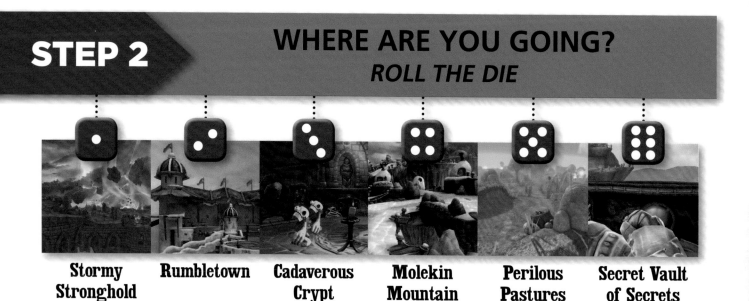

| Stormy Stronghold | Rumbletown | Cadaverous Crypt | Molekin Mountain | Perilous Pastures | Secret Vault of Secrets |

WHICH HAT ARE YOU TRYING TO FIND? *ROLL THE DIE*

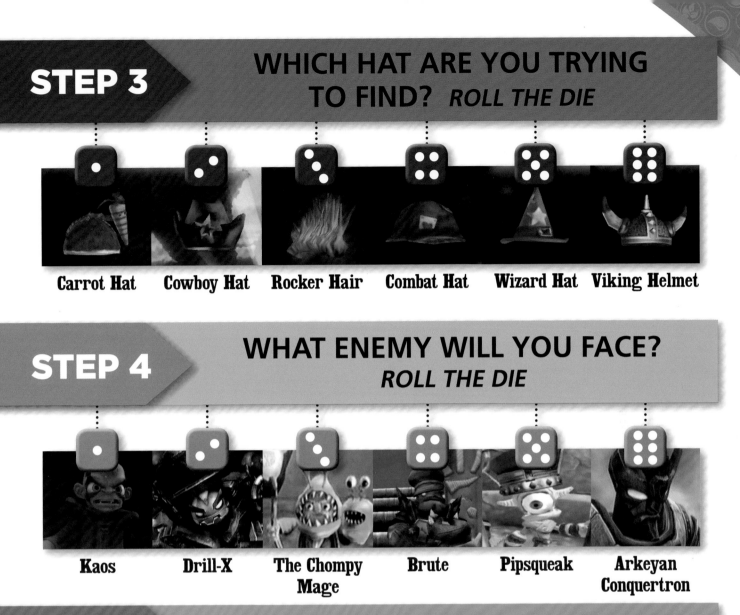

Carrot Hat   **Cowboy Hat**   **Rocker Hair**   **Combat Hat**   **Wizard Hat**   **Viking Helmet**

WHAT ENEMY WILL YOU FACE? *ROLL THE DIE*

Kaos   **Drill-X**   **The Chompy Mage**   **Brute**   **Pipsqueak**   **Arkeyan Conquertron**

WHAT MINIONS WILL THEY HAVE WORKING FOR THEM? *ROLL THE DIE*

Trolls   **Arkeyan Warriors**   **Drow**   **Cyclops**   **Spell Punks**   **Trogs**

YOUR MISSION

WRITE THE DETAILS OF YOUR ADVENTURE HERE

_____ will join me as I search _____ for the

_____ . But I'd better watch out 'cos _____ and

an army of _____ will be waiting for me.

GRIDLOCKED

1. TSHAPSUSMM
2. HBAS
3. RDNCYE
4. GRYPHITERAPG
5. RGINHOLDIGNT
6. GRINTOI
7. FELLAHTSTE
8. FINAGLERSMEL
9. EXH
10. RYPSO
11. MRWSA
12. AECVTJ

Oh no! While trying to rescue a friend from the clutches of Kaos, the Skylanders got mixed up in the evil Portal Master's Sinister and Super-Scary Scrambling Spell. Unscramble their names and fit them in the grid to see who they need to rescue.

THE SKYLANDERS' FRIEND IS:

FIRE AND WATER

HOW HOT IS YOUR MEMORY? LOOK AT THIS PAGE FOR A MINUTE AND
THEN TURN OVER AND SEE HOW MANY QUESTIONS YOU CAN ANSWER.
STAY COOL AND YOU'LL BE AMAZED HOW MUCH YOU'LL REMEMBER.

FIRE

WATER

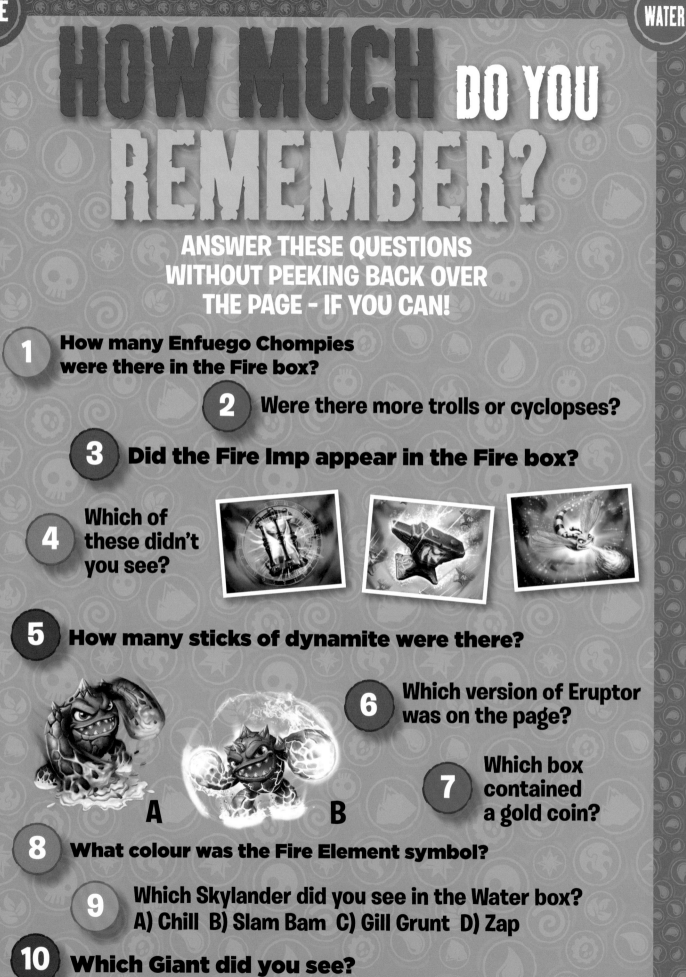

HOW MUCH DO YOU REMEMBER?

ANSWER THESE QUESTIONS WITHOUT PEEKING BACK OVER THE PAGE - IF YOU CAN!

1 How many Enfuego Chompies were there in the Fire box?

2 Were there more trolls or cyclopses?

3 Did the Fire Imp appear in the Fire box?

4 Which of these didn't you see?

5 How many sticks of dynamite were there?

6 Which version of Eruptor was on the page?

A   B

7 Which box contained a gold coin?

8 What colour was the Fire Element symbol?

9 Which Skylander did you see in the Water box?
A) Chill B) Slam Bam C) Gill Grunt D) Zap

10 Which Giant did you see?

INTERVIEW WITH A
GIANT

Water Giant Thumpback talks to Hugo about colossal crustaceans, pirate porridge and the fate of the Phantom Tide . . .

Hugo: Thumpback, you're best known for being one of the Giants, but you weren't always a Skylander. Is it true that you were once a pirate?

Thumpback: Yup, that's right. Served under Captain Frightbeard on the Phantom Tide. Signed up when I was just a tiddler.

H: Why did you want to become a pirate?

T: Two reasons really. I wanted to travel the 7,243 seas, have thrilling adventures and go fishing.

H: Er, that's three reasons.

T: Is it? Never been much good at sums, which was a pity as the Cap'n put me in charge of counting his booty. Big mistake.

H: Did you enjoy being a pirate?

T: Not really. The Phantom Tide was a bit on the titchy side even for a Giant ship. I could hardly stand up. And the food was dreadful. Stale sheep wool porridge every day. Yuck! And don't get me started on the poop deck . . .

H: Oh yes, I meant to ask. What is a poop deck?

T: You don't want to know. No, the biggest problem was that I didn't much like all the pillaging that goes with the job. All I wanted to do was fish.

H: And there was one particular sea creature you wanted to catch, wasn't there?

T: Indeed there was. The Leviathan Cloud Crab. Some people didn't even believe it existed. It has a shell the size of a house, and pincers that could snip a ship in two. Everywhere we sailed, I cast off in the hope of getting a nibble.

H: What bait did you use?

T: Sheep mostly. But sometimes the odd troll.

H: Did you ever catch it?

T: It caught me! There I was, sitting on the Tide's plank, when I felt a tug on me fishing line. The next thing I knew, I was being pulled overboard. I grabbed the ship's anchor, but the crab was so strong it yanked me away, anchor and all. Dragged halfway across Skylands, I was.

H: Did you ever see your crewmates again?

T: Well, here's the thing. Not long after, ol' Frightbeard got in a spot of bother with those rust-bucket Arkeyans. The Tide and all its crew were banished to the Chest of Exile for 10,000 years of nothing to eat but sheep-wool porridge. Lucky escape, if you ask me. Anyway, soon after that I signed up as a Skylander . . .

H: And helped defeat the Arkeyan King. Do you still find time to fish?

T: Whenever I can. In fact, I'm having another go at catching the Cloud Crab right now. Trouble is, I've run out of bait. 'Ere, you don't fancy hanging off this hook do you?

H: Why not? What's the worst that could happen?

Eye-Brawl's
Undead
Survival Guide

The undead can be a spooky old bunch, what with all that dark magic and gnashing teeth, and of course the strange smell of rotten candyfloss. Fortunately, Eye-Brawl is here with his grim guide to things that go bump in the night . . .

Huge pummelling fists

EYE-BRAWL
Here's proof that two Skylanders are better than one. Long ago, in the land of the Undead, a flying eyeball and a headless Giant were locked in a bitter rivalry. After over a century of fighting, the weird warriors realized that they could be truly unbeatable if they joined forces. The eyeball settled on the Giant's headless shoulders and Eye-Brawl was born.

Massive stomping feet

QUICK QUIZ
What is Eye-Brawl's battle cry?
A) The eyes have it!
B) I've got my eye on you!
C) Here's one in your eye!

One of the Trog Wanderers on this page is slightly different to the rest. Can you spot which one?

Eerie staring eye

6

Big eyes for seeing in the dark

THE TROUBLE WITH TROGS

Get the low-down on these loathsome ghouls

TROG WANDERERS

Eternally peckish, these slow-moving critters won't rest until they're nibbling on your arms, legs or any other body parts they can get their teeth into. Hit 'em and they shrink away to nothing.

Fiendish feathers

TROG PINCHERS

Trog pinchers make great pets. Well, as long as you like your pets to have super-sharp blades for hands and needle-like fangs, that is.

TROGMANDER

More intelligent than Trog Wanderers*, these menacing mages can transmogrify Trog Pinchers into GIANT Trog Pinchers. Giant angry Trog Pinchers at that.

BARK DEMON

One minute these wooden horrors look like normal trees, and the next they've sprouted hideous eyes, vicious mouths and grabbing arms. Trust me, their bite is worse than their bark.

BATTERSON'S PIES

Three cheers for Batterson! For years, ghosts only ate the brains of the living (with the odd soul ice cream for dessert). Then a Molekin baker called Batterson opened up a pie shop in Darklight Crypt. The ghosts went gaga for the pastry products and stopped eating brains for good. Now Batterson's pie shops are popping up all over Skylands.

3 WAYS TO SURVIVE A ROTTING ROBBIE ATTACK

1. Run. Robbies aren't exactly speedy – especially when bits of them keep falling off.

2. Produce a beef and onion pie from your back pocket (with extra gravy if you have it). They'll soon forget about eating you.

3. Whistle a funky tune. Zombies just love disco dancing. Why would they waste time biting you when they can get down and boogie instead?

* Actually, most stones are more intelligent than Trog Wanderers.

Arkeyan
Treasure Hunt

An ancient Arkeyan super weapon is buried deep beneath Crystal Eye Castle, but where should you start digging? Follow the clues to help Jet-Vac find it before Kaos does.

CLUES

Start your search at square **B8**

Move **3** squares down

Move **4** squares South West

Move **2** squares North

Move **3** squares West

Move **2** squares North East

Move **4** squares East

Move **3** squares South

True or False?

The Arkeyans created the Portals of Power.

☐ TRUE ☐ FALSE

On which square should you start digging?
MARK THE SPOT WITH AN X.

NINJINI'S MAGIC
MASTERCLASS

BECOME A MASTER (OR MISTRESS) OF MAGIC WITH THESE AMAZING TRICKS.

THE DISAPPEARING COIN

WHAT YOU NEED
2 pieces of the same coloured card
A handkerchief
A drinking glass
Sticky tape
A coin

WHAT HAPPENS?
You place a coin next to a glass, which is standing upside down on a sheet of coloured card. You cover the glass with a handkerchief and move it over the coin. When you've said the magic word you pull away the hankie and the coin has vanished.

HOW DOES IT WORK?
1. Before you perform the trick, trace the rim of the glass onto the sheet of card and cut out the circle.
2. Tape the circle carefully to the glass.
3. Now when you place it on the second sheet of card, the circle will completely blend in.
4. When you move the card over the secret circle of camouflaged card will hide the coin, making it look like it's disappeared.

THE FLOATING KETCHUP SACHET

WHAT YOU NEED
A sachet of ketchup
A plastic water bottle

WHAT HAPPENS?
You reveal a bottle of water. Inside lies a sachet of ketchup (like the ones you get in restaurants). Holding the bottle in your hand, you command the ketchup to rise and the sachet floats to the top. Tell it to dive and it sinks to the bottom. You have made the ketchup sachet move by the power of your mind.

HOW DOES IT WORK?
1. Before you put it into the bottle give the sachet a good old tweak, bending it around. This adds air bubbles to the sauce inside.
2. Pop it in the bottle and add water.
3. Hold the bottle in your hand and gently give it a squeeze. The change in water pressure makes the sachet rise.
4. Release the pressure on the bottle and the sachet will sink again.
5. Practise until you can get it to move without looking like you're squeezing the bottle.

49

Ship in a Bottle

by Onk Beakman

"Can that thing play rock music?" thundered Crusher, as the Dread-Yacht banked around a shoal of sky-salmon.

"The Octophonic Music Player can play anything you want," Flynn shouted, straining to be heard over the Molekin jazz that was blasting from the ship's music machine. "It's almost as impressive as me!"

"Shame you can't say the same about the rest of this rust bucket," said Sprocket, pulling herself out from under a control panel. "I've fixed the navi-tron, but your hyper-couplings are on the blink."

"Does nothing on this ship work properly?" asked Sonic Boom, touching down beside the Tech Skylander.

"It's that stupid curse," replied Sprocket. "Things break faster than I can fix 'em!"

"I've told you before," insisted Flynn. "The Dread-Yacht isn't cursed. She's just . . . WOAH!"

As if to prove the pilot wrong, the Octophonic went haywire. With a screech of feedback, the music machine started spewing out discs in every direction.

"You were saying?" commented Crusher, as he batted away an incoming disc with his hammer, but Flynn wasn't listening. He was just staring ahead, his eyes wide and glassy. He normally only looked like that when he was gazing into a mirror.

"What's wrong with him?" asked Sonic Boom as the deck lurched beneath her claws.

"Dunno," admitted Crusher, "but look what he's flying us into!"

The Giant was pointing at a huge, swirling whirlpool in the sky ahead.

"Ooh, pretty . . ." slurred Flynn as he sailed straight towards the middle of the multi-coloured maelstrom.

"He's in some kind of trance," yelled Sprocket. "Hang onto something. We're going in!"

The Dread-Yacht was dragged spinning into the storm.

"Ugh," groaned Flynn, finally coming around. "What happened?"

"You were hypnotized. That's what happened," said Sonic Boom. "And now we're . . . actually, where are we?"

"Somewhere real misty," growled Crusher. "Can't see a thing in the sky."

Sure enough, where once there was blue sky there was now dirty white nothingness. It was ominously quiet too – at least, it was until the silence was broken by a booming, disembodied voice.

"Glumshanks you FOOL. You could have chosen a cleaner bottle."

"Hey," started Flynn. "That sounded like . . ."

"Kaos!" Sonic Boom hissed.

The boat shook. At first it looked like the mist was clearing, but actually it was being wiped away by what appeared to be a gigantic sleeve. Flanked by Glumshanks and a horde of ugly trolls, a huge face stared down at them. Kaos' face.

Without hesitation, Sonic Boom shot into the air, flying straight towards the over-sized Portal Master. CRUNCH! The griffin slammed into an invisible wall just beyond Kaos' nose.

"What did you hit?" Crusher asked, catching her as she fell back to the deck.

"It was glass," replied Sonic Boom. "We're trapped in some kind of gigantic bottle."

"A tiny bottle you mean," crowed Kaos from above. "I, KAOS, have shrunk you down to down to size thanks to my SINISTER SECRET SHRINKING SPELL. You are DOOOOOOMED!"

"We'll see about that," shouted Sprocket, whipping up one of her guntowers and peppering the glass with shells. At the same time, Crusher chucked his hammer up towards Kaos, but had to duck as it ricocheted back at them. Sonic Boom even tried to shatter the glass with her voice, but just smashed every window in the Dread-Yacht.

"You'll never get through," cackled Kaos. "The Mystical Bottle of Miniaturization is UNBREAKABLE!"

Sprocket glanced at the shards of glass from the window and had an idea. Racing over to the wreckage of the Octophonic, she snatched up the music player's brass horn and ripped Flynn's intercom from the helm. Her hands blurred as she worked, combining the horn, the intercom and parts of her tower into a brand new machine.

"Sonic," she said, handing the griffin a microphone. "Scream into this."

"Uh-oh," said Crusher. "Cover your ears."

"Why?" asked a completely baffled Flynn. "What's gonna happen?"

"This!" Sonic screeched into Sprocket's gadget. Her super-sonic shriek was amplified by the machine, making every deck-plate rattle. Better still, the glass around the Dread-Yacht started to vibrate.

"What's THAAAT?" howled Kaos, clasping his hands over his ears.

"Lord Kaos," winced Glumshanks. "The bottle is about to . . ."

SMASH!

The glass prison disintegrated as Sonic's screech hit the right note. Released from Kaos' spell, the ship – and the Skylanders – began to grow.

"ATTACK, YOU FOOLS!" bellowed Kaos. "Quick, before they get too BIIIIG!"

Kaos' trolls rushed forward but it was hopeless. Even though they were still tiny, the Skylanders leapt from the growing boat. Sprocket whacked the trolls' ankles with her spanner, Crusher pummelled their toes and Sonic Boom shrieked into their ears. Within seconds the ever-expanding Dread-Yacht had filled Kaos' lair. Flynn gunned the engines.

"Grab hold of this," he said, releasing a rope ladder. "We're going to smash our way out."

As Kaos and Glumshanks ran for cover, the now full-size Dread-Yacht burst through the walls of Kastle Kaos.

The ship rocketed into the brilliant blue sky, the Skylanders still hanging from the ladder. Far below them, Kaos pulled himself out from under a pile of bricks.

"My beautiful castle," he wailed. "It's RUINED!"

"It's not that bad," said Glumshanks unconvincingly.

"NOT THAT BAD? IDIOT! There's a massive great hole in the wall!"

"Well, you've always said you wanted air conditioning," the troll offered with a shrug.

The End

EXCLUSIVE

WHO'S YOUR FAVOURITE SKYLANDER?

For the first time ever, the team behind the Skylanders games and books reveal who their favourite Skylanders are, and why . . .

I love **Chill** because she was a celebrated captain in the Snow Queen's guard!

Lindsay Friedman
Licensing & Partnerships Manager, Activision

CHILL

Flashwing is the perfect combatant and, once levelled up, she is unstoppable! She is both quick and agile, and can fight coming or going. Even in the rare moments when she has to retreat, she can still fire her crystal shards from behind, and take out her enemies as she high-tails it away. Her abilities are diverse too – she can twirl away a slew of Chompies in no time, or hit a Blaster Troll from a safe distance. She's also the perfect choice for completing Heroic Challenges! Her ability to shoot so precisely helps you hit even the smallest of targets (such as purple Chompies in 'Save the Purple Chompies') and not the things you're supposed to avoid. Flashwing is my go-to gal for getting things done! And here's a great fighting tip – if your Flashwing is levelled up, and you know an enemy is approaching, start shooting before they get there! Flashwing's crystals embed in walls and can fire on their own, so you can use her to set up your own ambushes for the bad guys!

Alex Ness
Chief of Staff, Toys For Bob

FLASHWING

Camo! He's a totally awesome looking dragon. That, and he grows watermelons, which are delicious! His firecracker vines upgrade into an awesome ranged attack that goes fast, surrounds your enemies and lays down sun blasts – all at the same time. Big time firepower!

Peter Kavic
Producer, Toys for Bob

CAMO

Flameslinger is the fastest Skylander in all of Skylands! Upgrade on the Pyromancer path and you can get the Supernova upgrade! This gives you a bigger blast ring when drawing a circle with the Flame Dash, which is devastating on large groups of enemies. Picking up the Napalm Tipped Arrows upgrade and Inferno Blast upgrades along this path makes your arrows do more damage from a distance when charged up for additional mayhem. Plus, upgrading to the Wow Pow Speed Demon upgrade will increase the speed of your Flame Dash, making Flameslinger one of the fastest Skylanders so you can speed through levels with ease.

Chris Bruno
QA–Manager, Toys for Bob

FLAMESLINGER

It's **Double Trouble** for me. His attacks are great for any occasion and he has a hilarious personality. You can also utilize all of his abilities in different ways. His main attack (the Eldritch Beam) is awesome against big enemies, and you are able to 'lock-on' so you can fire at an enemy while circling around them and dodging their attacks. The 'Doubles' that he can summon are a great way to pummel enemies even while fleeing, as they will go on the attack even when you aren't there. Oh, and the Magic Bomb attack is a great way to clear out low health enemies in one action (like a wave of pesky Chompies, for example!). All together, Double Trouble has three great moves that can be utilized in any situation. Boom-Shock-A-Laka!!!

Lou Studdert
Production Coordinator, Skylanders Giants™

DOUBLE TROUBLE

Chop Chop! But my first love will always be Spyro.

Mike Graham
Design Producer, Skylanders Giants™

CHOP CHOP!

Definitely **Trigger Happy** . . . because he's 'mine, mine, mine!' Try his Pot O' Gold upgrade – if it lands on heads, it does even MORE damage!

Tyler Everett
Production Coordinator, Skylanders Giants™

TRIGGER HAPPY

When I adventure through Skylands, I always keep **Terrafin** within reach. His Earth Swim burrowing ability allows him to sneak up on enemies and take the bite out of the competition. It's Feeding Time!

Scott Murata
International Licensing and Partnerships, Activision

TERRAFIN

It's got to be **Zap**. He has the speed to circle around all types of enemies in order to avoid being attacked. While weaving through enemies, he can use his Lightning Breath to not just deal damage, but also temporarily stun his foes. Use his Sea Slime Slide to weave around and leave a slime trail that will stop enemies in their tracks. Once upgraded, you can shoot the slime trails with your Lightning Breath, causing them to become electrified. At this point, if any enemies become stuck on the slime trail, they also get shocked! You can also use Zap's speed to your advantage. Keep a distance from your enemies and light them up using your Lightning Breath!

Elias Jimenez
Associate Producer, Skylanders Giants™

ZAP

Stealth Elf! She's fast and deadly, and with her health regeneration ability she can survive the Arena Challenges better than most.

Shin Ohyama
Producer, Toys For Bob

STEALTH ELF

Slam Bam is my personal favourite. It's a combination of his moves and his personality that puts him at the top of my list. His bruising melee punch combos are effective on their own, but what I really like to do is freeze enemies at a distance, use the Yeti Ice Shoe Slide to get up close and then unleash a mighty barrage of punches. Finally, the frosty icing on the cake is the ability to traverse water areas on his surfboard.

Toby Schadt
Lead Designer, Toys For Bob

SLAM BAM

...AND WHAT ABOUT THE TEAM WHO WORK ON THE BOOKS?

Hot Dog! What's not to love about this molten mutt? If his Firebark wasn't fierce enough, his Wall of Fire can get any enemy hot under the collar. Plus, he's always burning with such enthusiasm. The pyrotechnic pup is just so persistent, always ready to bound into action. Good dog!

Cavan Scott
Writer

HOT DOG

My favourite seems to change pretty much every time I play, but at the moment I've got some serious love for **Jet-Vac**. With his Suction Gun he doesn't have to mess around chasing after enemies – he makes them come to him! I still hate doing the vacuuming though.

Gary Panton
Editor

JET-VAC

The other Skylanders may find it funny that he calls everyone 'sir', but I like **Drill Sergeant's** loyalty. Being able to shoot out Drill Rockets while charging towards enemies at full speed isn't too bad either! A real solid guy to have around.

James Evans
Designer

DRILL SERGEANT

Sometimes I can't decide which Skylander to use – which makes **Pop Fizz** perfect, as he's two Skylanders in one! One moment he's a fuzzy blue gremlin, and the next he's a beastly berserker – perfect!

Kirstie Billingham
Art Director

POP FIZZ

CREATE YOUR OWN SKYLANDER

Now that you've read about which Skylanders the team love best, how about designing your own? Have a go at conjuring your own champion.

 **STEP 1** WHICH ELEMENT WILL THEY BE?

 **STEP 2** WHAT SPECIAL POWER WILL THEY HAVE?

Can you think of something completely new that would make your Skylander stand out?

 **STEP 3** WHAT WAS THEIR STORY BEFORE THEY WERE A SKYLANDER?

I-Wei Huang, who has the cool job of designing Skylanders, shares some of his top secret tips:

1. "Draw and draw and draw. Try to do as many things with your character as possible, drawing them from every angle."

2. "Don't settle on one thing. Keep experimenting. If you've thought about a dragon who breathes fire, keep the power but change the character. He needn't spit fire, he could throw it instead. Be as creative as possible."

3. "Show your character to a bunch of people. If it makes them chuckle or go 'woah', you know you're on to something. You want to get a reaction from them.

DRAW YOUR SKYLANDER HERE  STEP4

WHAT IS YOUR SKYLANDER'S NAME? STEP5

Think you've created a really cool Skylander? Why not send it to the Skylanders Annual team at skylanders@uk.penguingroup.com? We'll show off our favourites in next year's Annual!

59

The Oracle's Trial of Knowledge

Skylands' Oracle knows all things. Do you? Take the Oracle's quiz to find out. *Good luck!*

Trial 1: The Easy Path

1 WHEN DID THE ARKEYANS RULE SKYLANDS?
a) 1,000 years ago
b) 10,000 years ago
c) 100,000 years ago

2 WHICH OF THESE SKYLANDERS DOESN'T BELONG TO THE LIFE ELEMENT?

3 WHAT WAS THE POWER SOURCE OF THE ARKEYAN KING?
a) The Steel Fist of Arkus
b) The Iron Fist of Arkus
c) The Jelly Fist of Arkus

4 FRIGHT RIDER RIDES A . . .
a) Skeletal sparrow
b) Skeletal parrot
c) Skeletal ostrich

5 WHO IS THIS?
a) Hugo
b) Blobbers
c) Snuckles

6 WHAT KIND OF GIANT IS HOT HEAD?
a) Fire
b) Water
c) Earth

7 WHICH OF THE FOLLOWING ISN'T A TYPE OF SKYLANDS CREATURE?
a) Molekin
b) Wheely Bin
c) Wilikin

Trial 2:
The Trickier Path

8 NAME FLYNN'S ONE TRUE LOVE (OTHER THAN HIMSELF, THAT IS).
a) Stealth Elf
b) Cali
c) Chill

9 WHICH GIANT HAS BEEN SCRAMBLED BY THIS ELEMENTAL GATE?

10 WHAT IS JET-VAC?
a) An Air Baron
b) A Wing Baron
c) A Sky Baron

11 WHO RUNS CUTTHROAT CARNIVAL?
a) Pirates
b) Trolls
c) Drow

12 WHAT IS THE NAME OF THE SKYLANDERS WHO CAN SWAP THEIR TOPS AND BOTTOMS?
a) Swap Soldiers
b) SWAP Force
c) Swaplanders

13 WHAT DOES AURIC NORMALLY WEAR?
a) Pyjamas
b) A suit
c) A cowboy outfit

14 WHAT DO THE WILIKINS CALL KAOS?
a) The Maker
b) The Baker
c) That bald bloke

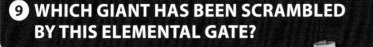

Trial 3:
The Blooming Difficult Path

15 WHAT IS THE NAME OF CRUSHER'S HAMMER?

16 WHAT KIND OF CREATURE IS SPROCKET?

17 WHAT IS THE ORACLE'S REAL NAME?

18 WHAT IS WRONG WITH THIS PICTURE OF EON?

19 HOW MANY TOES DOES GLUMSHANKS HAVE ON EACH FOOT?

20 KAOS OWES TERRAFIN SOME MONEY. HOW MUCH?

HOW DID YOU DO?

0-4 answers correct
Oh dear, Portal Master. Your lack of knowledge is worrying. I'd visit Hugo's library if I were you.

5-15 answers correct
A fine effort. You are most certainly on the road to wisdom.

16-20 answers correct
A stupendous effort. Well done. Your knowledge rivals mine. In fact, I'm in real need of a holiday. You don't fancy being the Oracle for a bit, do you?

61

ANSWERS

PAGE 7
True or False?: **False. They were Molekin tilers.**

Ermit is found on **page 30**

PAGE 8-9
True or False?: **True**

PAGE 14-15
True or False?: **False. He used Bomb Fiends.**

PAGE 16-17
SKYLANDS SEARCH

PAGE 20
LETHAL LABYRINTH

PAGE 24
HOME SWEET HOME
Terrafin – Dirt Seas
Jet-Vac – Windham
Hot Dog – Popcorn Volcano

Shroomboom – Kaos' Pizza Topping Garden
Swarm – The Honeycomb Pyramid
Lightning Rod – Cloud Kingdom
Chill – The Ice Kingdom

True or False? **False. It was the Ice Queen.**

PAGE 28-29
CREATURE FEATURE
The character who isn't a bad guy is Quigley.

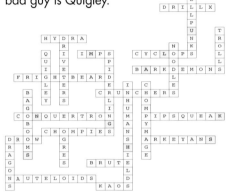

GLUMSHANKS

PAGE 32
TECH TILE
The message reads:
Sprocket used to fix her uncle's mad inventions when she was growing up

PAGE 37
CODE NAMES
The answer is **Glacier Gully**

PAGE 38
POTION PUZZLER
D and H are the same.

PAGE 42
GRIDLOCKED
The Skylanders' friend is:

¹STUMPSMASH
²BASH
³CYNDER
⁴TRIGGERHAPPY
⁵LIGHTNINGROD
⁶IGNITOR
⁷STEALTHELF
⁸FLAMESLINGER
⁹HEX
¹⁰SPYRO
¹¹SWARM
¹²JETVAC

PAGE 44
FIRE AND WATER
1. Three
2. There were more cyclopses
3. No
4. The Hourglass
5. Three
6. Version A
7. Fire
8. Red
9. Slam Bam
10. Hot Head

PAGE 46-47
QUICK QUIZ
B) I've got my eye on you!
Trog Wanderer number 5 is the only one with red eyes.

PAGE 48
TREASURE HUNT
Start digging in box **H7**
True or False: **False. Nobody knows who created the Portals.**

PAGES 60-61
THE ORACLE'S TRIAL OF KNOWLEDGE
1. b) 10,000 years ago
2. Wrecking Ball
3. b) The Iron Fist of Arkus
4. c) Skeletal ostrich
5. a) Hugo
6. a) Fire
7. b) Wheely Bin
8. b) Cali
9. Ninjini
10. c) A Sky Baron
11. a) Pirates
12. b) SWAP Force
13. b) A suit
14. a) The Maker
15. Crusher
16. A Golding
17. Octavius Cloptimus
18. He has brown eyes
19. Four
20. Five dollars